J 277.1 Lap

Lappin, M.
The church

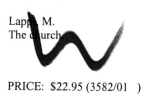

PRICE: $22.95 (3582/01   )

W9-ARQ-383

TOWN OF CALEDON PUBLIC LIBRARY

The Church

by Megan Lappi

WEIGL EDUCATIONAL PUBLISHERS LIMITED

TOWN OF CALEDON PUBLIC LIBRARY

Published by Weigl Educational Publishers Limited
6325-10 Street SE
Calgary, Alberta
Canada T2H 2Z9
Web site: www.weigl.com

Copyright 2005 WEIGL EDUCATIONAL PUBLISHERS LIMITED
All rights reserved. No part of this publication may be reproduced, stored in a retrieval system, or transmitted in any form or by any means, electronic, mechanical, photocopying, recording, or otherwise, without the prior written permission of Weigl Educational Publishers Limited.

Library and Archives Canada Cataloguing in Publication Data

Lappi, Megan
     The church / Megan Lappi.

(Early Canadian life)
Includes index.
ISBN 1-55388-060-9 (bound).--ISBN 1-55388-092-7 (pbk.)

    1. Canada--Church history--Juvenile literature.
2. Pioneers--Religious life--Canada--Juvenile literature.
3. Frontier and pioneer life--Canada--Juvenile literature.
I. Title. II. Series: Early Canadian life (Calgary, Alta.)

BR570.L36 2004   j277.1   C2004-904097-9

Printed and bound in the United States of America
1 2 3 4 5 6 7 8 9 0 09 08 07 06 05 04

We acknowledge the financial support of the Government of Canada through the Book Publishing Industry Development Program (BPIDP) for our publishing activities.

Photograph Credits
Every reasonable effort has been made to trace ownership and to obtain permission to reprint copyright material. The publishers would be pleased to have any errors or omissions brought to their attention so that they may be corrected in subsequent printings.
Cover: Glenbow Archives: main (NA-1633-20), **Photos.com:** background; **Barrett & MacKay Photography Inc.:** pages 11, 19, 23L; **Ellen Bryan:** pages 8, 22; **Glenbow Archives:** pages 3B (NA-2488-4), 5 (NA-2328-2), 6 (NA-1687-36), 7 (NA-1135-32), 9 (NA-2283-1), 10 (NA-3562-3), 14T (NA-2502-13), 15T (NA-2003-104), 15M (NA-2755-9), 15B (NA-1604-54), 16 (NA-3649-1), 17 (NA-2488-4), 18 (NA-1946-5); **McCord Museum of Canadian History, Montreal:** pages 4 (M656 Old Bonsecours Church), 12 (MP-0000.2360.49 Pulpit and harmonium, ca.1900), 14B (MP-0000.2360.51 Congregation in church, ca.1900); **Photos.com:** pages 3T, 13T, 13B; **Rose Schwartzenberger:** pages 1, 20, 23R.

Project Coordinator
Tina Schwartzenberger

Design
Janine Vangool

Layout
Jeff Brown

Substantive Editor
Heather Kissock

Photo Researcher
Ellen Bryan

Contents

Introduction

In many pioneer towns, the church was an important place. It was often the centre of activity. People gathered at churches to worship. They attended **sermons**. Children went to Sunday school at the church. Most weddings, **baptisms**, funerals, and other religious ceremonies were held at the church. Some pioneers travelled long distances to attend church services.

Pioneers in Montreal began attending church services at Notre-Dame-de-Bonsecours in 1817.

In 1888, the North-West Mounted Police band played music at a church picnic in Lethbridge, Alberta. Few churches had bands or choirs at that time.

The church was also used for non-religious community events. These events included picnics, music concerts, and **bazaars**. People gathered at the church to have fun. The church was also a place where people could meet their neighbours. During the nineteenth century, few women worked outside their homes. Neighbours often lived far apart. The church gave women a chance to meet and talk to other women in the community.

Did you know:

People follow many different religions. People of all religions meet in special places to worship.

A Place of Worship

The whole community was usually excited about building the church. Everyone helped build the church. Churches were built using materials that were available in the area. Early churches may have been made from logs. If the community had a sawmill, the church was built with wood that had been cut at the sawmill. Sometimes churches were built with bricks and stones. On the prairies, some churches even had roofs made from blocks of earth and grass called sod.

Church buildings were many different sizes, both big and small, across Canada. Usually, the size of a church depended on the number of people living in the community.

Communities in early Canada were often far apart. Saddleback preachers served many communities across a large area.

Most towns did not have a priest or minister living in their community. Instead, one priest, minister, or rabbi provided religious guidance to several towns in an area. These religious leaders were sometimes called "circuit riders" or "saddleback preachers" because they rode horses between communities. Other priests and ministers travelled on foot or in canoes. If a town did not have a church, services were held in schoolhouses, general stores, or in people's homes.

Did you know:

The oldest church in Canada is Notre-Dame-des-Victoires in Quebec City. It was built in 1688.

First-hand account:

A Presbyterian student minister, T. J. S. Ferguson, remembers what being a saddleback preacher was like.

In those days, we all travelled by horseback and 40 miles on a Sunday with three preaching services was quite common. The Prairie was lovely, the air clean, the Rockies inspiring, and the people **hospitable**.

Church Leaders

As a town grew, the community hired a priest, minister, or rabbi to lead religious services. This person often lived in a house next to the church. The house was called a parsonage, rectory, or manse. If the town did not have a church, the priest, minister, or rabbi might live in their own home. Sometimes, religious leaders **boarded** with a family in the area. Women in the church often raised money from people in the town to help pay the leader's salary.

The community had to build the church leader's home. Often, people from two or three towns built the home together to save money.

The first religious people to come to Canada were Jesuit **missionaries**. The Jesuits belonged to a religious organization called the Society of Jesus. Jesuits built missions, or religious communities.

Priests, ministers, and rabbis were very important people in early Canadian communities. They visited the sick and poor, baptized babies and young children, married couples, and said prayers at funerals. People in the community asked their church leaders for guidance.

The first Canadian pioneers welcomed any religious leader who came to their community. In the second half of the nineteenth century, pioneers wanted religious leaders who shared their beliefs.

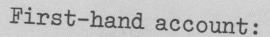

First-hand account:

Reverend E. Davidge remembers his early years as a minister on the prairies:

My salary was $600 per year, with an additional $75 for horse-keep. I had the use of two horses while on the Mission, a grey-white one called Dick, and, later, a chestnut that Reverend Bowen loaned me.

Going to Church

Going to church was a special occasion. Families dressed in their "Sunday best" clothing. Women and girls wore dresses, gloves, and hats. Men and boys wore their nicest clothes and freshly polished boots to church. Women left their hats on in church. Men and boys removed their hats before they entered the church. Removing their hats was a sign of respect.

Pioneers did not have many clothes. Most pioneers only had one outfit to wear to church.

Women often made all the clothing for their families. Sometimes, they had to make cloth from wool. Old flour or sugar sacks were made into dresses for girls and women.

Many people lived far from church on farms and **homesteads** in the country. These families travelled to church in horse-drawn wagons in the summer and in sleds in the winter. Families that lived in town walked to church. After the service, people left the church quietly. Children could not run and play, laugh, or talk loudly.

Did you know:

In early Canada, people were not allowed to work on Sundays. Sunday was a day of worship. Everyone was expected to attend church.

First-hand account:

One church leader shares his memories of pioneers arriving for church services:

It always thrilled me to see the people coming to Worship from all directions in buggies, **democrates**, or by saddle.

Tools of the Church Leader

The items found in a church 100 years ago are similar to those found in churches today. Many historic churches have changed little and are still used today.

Pulpit

In many churches, the priest, minister, or rabbi stands on the pulpit during the sermon. The pulpit is a raised platform at the front of the church. Before churches were built, people used whatever materials or items they could find. Sometimes a box was used as a pulpit. In many early churches, the pulpits were made from wood.

Holy Books

Most religions have a holy book. This book explains the stories and rules of the religion. During a sermon, parts of the book were read to the **congregation**. The priest, minister, or rabbi explained what the stories and rules meant. Some holy books have changed very little from the ones that were used in the 1800s.

Pews

Pews are the rows of seats found in a church. Pews were made from different materials, depending on how much money the community had. In the 1800s, people might sit on benches of hard pine wood with straight backs. In Wawota, Saskatchewan, people sat on wagon seats.

A Day in the Life

Church services were held at different times and on different days. For example, Christian services were usually held on Sundays. Jewish services were usually held on Saturdays. Here is what a Sunday church service might have been like for people in an early Canadian community more than 100 years ago.

8:00 a.m.

After breakfast on Sunday morning, everyone dressed carefully. They wanted to look their best. People who had a long way to travel left early. They went to church on wagons or sleds. A clean blanket was placed on the wagon seat so that clean Sunday clothes would not get dirty. In town, many people walked along the edges of the streets, away from the dust.

11:00 a.m.

Just before the service began, everyone entered the church quietly and found a place to sit in a pew. Families usually sat together, all in a row. People might smile or nod to greet their neighbours, but no one spoke. Church services began at 11:00 a.m.

1:30 p.m.

The morning sermon usually lasted for about one hour. People who lived in town went home for lunch. Some families brought a picnic lunch if they lived farther away. In the afternoon, children returned to the church for Sunday school lessons.

6:00 p.m.

After Sunday school lessons, families ate supper. If their church was serving a meal, they would eat at the church. The women of the church cooked food for everyone. Some families cooked at home and brought food to the church.

8:00 p.m.

Evening services became popular as towns grew. Evening services were an important part of the community's social life. They were usually less **solemn** and attracted more people than morning services. Some evening services included music, singing, reading from the holy book, and a sermon. Natural gas lights helped people find their way to and from the church.

Sunday School

Halifax held Sunday school classes in 1783. Still, Sunday school did not become popular until the 1800s. Early Sunday schools were very much like the Sunday schools of today. A church teacher read to children from the church's holy book. Sometimes children had to memorize verses, or sections, from their church's holy book.

Sunday schools mostly taught religion. Students also practised their reading skills in Sunday school.

Only children attended Sunday school, but the entire family attended the Sunday school picnic.

Many churches held a Sunday school picnic every summer. Most members of the community attended the picnics. Children played games like "tug of war." They would also drink lemonade and eat homemade ice cream.

Did you know:

In the early days, Sunday school was called "Sabbath Day School." Sabbath is the day of the week used for worship.

First-hand account:

One woman remembers the best part about her Sunday school in the early 1900s:

Sunday school was held after church in those days and when it was over Mrs. Bowman came around to all the children, young and older, to distribute peanuts and jelly beans.

Women and Church Events

Women were active in early church congregations across the country. Women created groups such as the Ladies' Aid, the Ladies' Auxiliary, and the Sewing Society. With the help of these womens' groups, the church held many events. Money raised was used to keep the church looking nice, to buy new furniture, and to help poor people in the community.

Some Ladies Aid groups had many members. The number of group members usually depended on how many people lived in the community.

For some occasions, such as Thanksgiving, the Ladies Aid decorated the church.

First-hand account:

One man wrote a poem to thank the women of the Ladies Aid for their work:

An appreciation—by a man

To those who knit, and those who sew
To those who quilt, and those who bake
To those who work and those who wait
On hungry folk at suppers hot
And suppers cold—it takes a lot
To raise the funds that needed are
To do the work both near and far
So here's our thanks, and wishes true
We bring them now, at last, to you.

Did you know:

Often, women paid for the materials to build a church and the furniture that went inside. Women raised the money by holding church suppers and bazaars.

Women organized most special events held at the church. Many people in the community attended church socials, choir practice, Christmas concerts, dances, picnics, and annual fall suppers. Christmas, Easter, and Thanksgiving were especially important occasions for Canadian pioneers. All of these events made the church the centre of social life for the community. Canada's early settlers worked very hard. They had little time for fun. Church events provided relief from the hard work of their everyday lives.

Churches Past and Present

People still attend church services in some of Canada's historic churches. Most churches today are large buildings. Churches today have carpets, stained-glass windows, and beautiful wooden pulpits and pews. People still come to church for the same reasons they did long ago—to worship.

Church Rules

Which of the church rules would apply to children today and children from the 1800s? Which rules would only apply to children in early Canada?

Go to Sunday school.

Wear a bonnet or hat if you are a girl.

Keep quiet during the sermon.

Take off your hat before you enter the church if you are a boy.

Some churches today are built to look like old churches. Others, like the Baptist Church in Watrous, Saskatchewan, look modern.

Then

Early Churches

- Families get to church by walking, horse-drawn sled, or wagon
- People wear their best clothes to church services
- One priest, minister, or rabbi travels to many communities
- People may attend more than one church service per day

- Everyone says prayers
- Families go to church once a week
- Children go to Sunday school
- Everyone sings hymns

Now

Today's Churches

- People usually get to church by car
- Some people dress up for church services and some wear casual clothes
- Most churches have at least one priest, minister, or rabbi
- People do not attend more than one church service per day

DIAGRAM

There are many differences between pioneer churches and churches today. There are some similarities between the two as well. The diagram on the left compares these similarities and differences. Copy the diagram in your notebook. Try to think of other similarities and differences to add to your diagram.

As you can see by the diagram, churches today have some things in common with churches 100 years ago.

Preserving the Past

St. Martin's Anglican Church

Many of Canada's old churches still exist. These buildings have been preserved so that people can see what churches were like many years ago. Some of these churches have been turned into museums. Others are still used as churches. A few of Canada's historic churches are shown on the map on the next page. Do you recognize any of them? Can you think of another church that could be added to the map?

1 Shrine Church
Martyrs' Shrine
Midland, ON

2 Notre-Dame Basilica
Montreal, QB

3 Anglican Cathedral of
St. John the Baptist
St. John's, NF

4 Mission of St.
Antoine de Padou
Batoche, SK

5 Congregation
Emanu-el Temple
Victoria, BC

6 Her Majesty's/St.
Paul's Chapel of
the Mohawks
Brantford, ON

7 Holy Trinity Church
Saskatoon, SK

8 Little Dutch
Church
Halifax, NS

9 St. Michael's
Ukrainian Greek
Orthodox Church
near Gardenton, MB

10 Notre-Dame-
des-Victoires
Quebec City, QB

11 Nazrey African
Methodist
Episcopal Church
Amherstburg, ON

12 All Saints Anglican Church
Watrous, SK

13 St. Martin's Anglican Church
*Heritage Park Historical Village,
Calgary, AB*

14 Acadian Church
North Barachois, NB

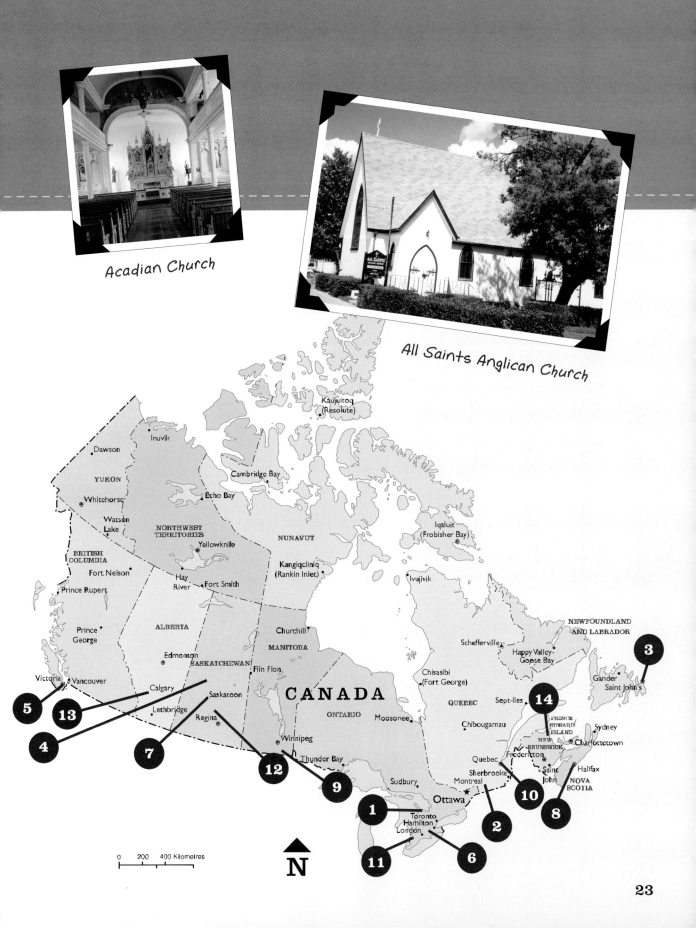

Acadian Church

All Saints Anglican Church

Glossary

Baptisms: religious ceremonies in which people are admitted to a Christian church

Bazaars: sales of many different items to raise money

Boarded: lived and ate meals at another person's house

Congregation: the people present at a religious service

Democrates: four-wheeled carriages with two double seats, one behind the other, pulled by two horses

Homesteads: parcels of land in the Canadian West granted to a settler by the government

Hospitable: making a visitor feel welcome

Missionaries: people sent by a church on a religious mission

Sermons: public talks about religion, given by a church leader

Solemn: serious and formal

Index